D0824710

UNDERSTANDING THE PARANORMAL

INVESTIGATING WITCHES AND WITCHCRAFT

THERESE SHEA

Britannica
Educational Publishing

IN ASSOCIATION WITH

ROSEN
EDUCATIONAL SERVICES

Published in 2015 by Britannica Educational Publishing (a trademark of Encyclopædia Britannica, Inc.) in association with The Rosen Publishing Group, Inc. 29 East 21st Street, New York, NY 10010

Distributed exclusively by Rosen Publishing.
To see additional Britannica Educational Publishing titles, go to rosenpublishing.com.

First Edition

Britannica Educational Publishing
J. E. Luebering: Director, Core Reference Group
Anthony L. Green: Editor, Compton's by Britannica

Rosen Publishing
Hope Lourie Killcoyne: Executive Editor
Heather Moore Niver: Editor
Nelson Sá: Art Director
Nicole Russo: Designer
Cindy Reiman: Photography Manager
Karen Huang: Photo Researcher

Library of Congress Cataloging-in-Publication Data

Shea, Therese.
Investigating witches and witchcraft/Therese Shea.—First Edition.
        pages cm.—(Understanding the paranormal)
Includes bibliographical references and index.
ISBN 978-1-62275-877-7 (library bound) — ISBN 978-1-62275-878-4 (pbk.) —
ISBN 978-1-62275-879-1 (6-pack)
1. Witchcraft. 2. Witches. 3. Wicca. I. Title.
BF1566.S445 2014
133.4'3—dc23

2014024103

Manufactured in the United States of America

Photo Credits:
Cover, p. 1 Maksim Shmeljov/Shutterstock.com; p. 5 MGM Studios/Moviepix/Getty Images; p. 7 © Walt Disney Pictures/Entertainment Pictures/ZUMA Press; p. 8 New Line/WireImage/Getty Images; p. 10 Frank and Frances Carpenter Collection/Library of Congress, Washington, D.C.; p. 13 Photos.com/Thinkstock; p. 14 ClassicStock.com/SuperStock; pp. 17, 19 De Agostini Picture Library/Getty Images; p. 20 The Bridgeman Art Library/Getty Images; p. 22 MPI/Archive Photos/Getty Images; p. 25 Xavier Arnau/Vetta/Getty Images; p. 27 Photononstop/Superstock; p. 28 Stubblefield Photography/Shutterstock.com; p. 30 © Kirk Condy/The Image Works; p. 31 Erin Paul Donovan/age fotostock/Getty Images; p. 33 David Q. Cavagnaro/Photolibrary/ Getty Images; pp. 36–37 © Warner Bros. Entertainment. All rights reserved/Courtesy Everett Collection; p. 38 Kittisuper/E+/Getty Images; p. 40 © Walt Disney Studios Motion Pictures/Courtesy Everett Collection; p. 42 Liquidlibrary/Thinkstock; interior pages background images © iStockphoto.com/ Kivilvim Pinar, © iStockphoto.com/mitja2.

CONTENTS

INTRODUCTION

Many young people are first introduced to the world of witches with the famous line from the movie *The Wizard of Oz*: "I'll get you, my pretty, and your little dog, too!" The line is uttered by the Wicked Witch of the West. With her green skin, pointy hat, and magical powers, she has many characteristics that people think of when they imagine witches.

But stories of witches and witchcraft were around thousands of years before this 1939 movie and the book upon which it is based. In fact, witchcraft, or rather the belief in it, has shaped some major events in history, often at a terrible cost in human life—as illustrated by the European witch hunts and the Salem witch trials.

Witchcraft is not, however, a practice only from history and fiction. Some cultures around the world still believe in witchcraft today. There is also a modern Western movement called Wicca that embraces some benevolent (kind and helpful) aspects of the magical art.

The actress Margaret Hamilton became famous for her portrayal of the Wicked Witch of the West in The Wizard of Oz. Hamilton is shown here in makeup and costume.

CHAPTER ONE

THE WORLD OF WITCHCRAFT

From the Wicked Witch of the West to the many witches of the *Harry Potter* series of books and films, there are numerous examples of good and bad witches in literature, movies, and other parts of popular culture. Though creations of someone's imagination, all these shape people's ideas of what witchcraft is. However, the stereotypical image of a cackling old woman flying around on a broomstick has little to do with the historical or modern practice of witchcraft.

WHAT'S WITCHCRAFT?

"Witchcraft" refers to the activity of witches: people alleged to use supernatural powers in the form of magic to influence people or events. The term "sorcery" has long been synonymous with witchcraft in the English-speaking world. Nevertheless, some scholars distinguish witchcraft from sorcery by noting that witches are usually regarded as possessing natural magical powers, whereas sorcerers are ordinary people using learned techniques.

Other scholars, noting that modern witches claim to learn their craft, suggest that sorcery's intent is always evil and that of witchcraft can be either good or bad. Historically, some people feared witches, believing their powers stemmed from

Tilda Swinton portrays the White Witch in the film The Chronicles of Narnia: The Lion, the Witch and the Wardrobe, *which is based on the book by C.S. Lewis.*

the devil or evil spirits. Today, in Western popular culture and especially in children's literature, the sorcerer often has a positive character, while witches are often malevolent, or evil.

Gandalf, the good wizard of The Hobbit *and* The Lord of the Rings *books and movies, is just one of the many magical beings, both benevolent and malevolent, of Middle-earth. The live-action film version of Gandalf is played by Ian McKellen, pictured here.*

Witches are often described in Western books and movies as being women, especially old women. However, people practicing or accused of practicing witchcraft have included both women and men of various ages.

WHAT'S A WARLOCK?

"Warlock" is one name for a man who practices witch-craft. The term may come from the Old English word *waerloga*, meaning "oath-breaker," which is why it is not a term often used positively. Male witches are also some-times called sorcerers or wizards—or simply witches. "Wizard" comes from a word meaning "wise." Some people use the label "warlock" to mean a wizard with stronger and more complex powers.

WITCH POWERS AND METHODS

Let's look at the powers associated with witchcraft and what it means to "influence people and events." Witch-craft has been thought to control death and disease, feel-ings of love and hate, crop failure and success, and the weather. Although some events attributed to witchcraft

The Maori people historically believed in makutu, or witchcraft. The group of Maori warriors shown here is performing the haka, a war dance displaying strength and unity.

might otherwise be considered "bad luck," other supposed feats of witchcraft are more extreme and fantastic, such as the transformation of people into animals. It is said that a witch might bring about some of these happenings through spells, sometimes called incantations.

Spells are words spoken in a certain way with magical intent. The correct recitation, often with gestures, is thought to unleash supernatural power. Some societies believe that incorrect recitation can not only cancel the magic but also cause the death of the reciter. The language of spells is sometimes archaic and not always understood. Much magical language, however, is directly linked with the aim of the spell in a poetic way. An example is a Maori spell giving speed and grace to a canoe, which speaks of the swiftness of a flying bird and the lightness of a sea gull.

Witches are also associated with blessings and curses, which are verbal expressions similar to spells. Certain gestures as well as words may be bound up with the act of blessing, as in putting one's hands on the head of the person being blessed. The curse, a wish to cause harm or misfortune, is usually directed against others. However, a form of curse associated with oaths, contracts, and treaties is directed against oneself if one lies or fails to keep a promise.

People practicing witchcraft have used a variety of other means to attempt to achieve their goals as well. These include divination, amulets and charms, dolls or other figures to represent enemies, and potions.

POTIONS

In witchcraft, a potion is a mixture of liquids believed to possess magical properties. A witch may give someone a medicinal potion to drink, for example, to cure him or her of an illness. Other potions are intended to cause harm. Common types of potions include love potions and sleeping potions. Potion-making was associated with alchemy, which was an early form of chemistry attempting to change base metals into gold, to discover a universal cure for disease, and to find a way to prolong life. Medieval healers used potions in their remedies. Over time, however, potions acquired an evil reputation.

WITCH IMAGERY

Witches are often pictured in modern Western portrayals as evil, cackling old women gathered around a boiling cauldron brewing potions. Cauldrons were once common cooking vessels. A group of women gathered around a large pot to cook could be perceived as suspicious and even evil if someone thought they were making potions. William Shakespeare's play *Macbeth* made this idea popular through his three witch characters, the Weird Sisters, who use animal parts to concoct a potion

This painting is an artist's depiction of the Weird Sisters, or the Three Witches, of Macbeth. The play's main character, Macbeth, is shown in the upper left.

in a cauldron. As they do so, they murmur the famous incantation: "Double, double toil and trouble; Fire burn, and cauldron bubble."

This kind of image is now instantly recognized as a witch. However, the black cat, pointed ha[t] and flying broomstick symbols have not always been associated with witches and witchcraft.

Drawings of witches wearing their now-famous pointy hats first began to appear in children's books in England in the early 1700s. Scholars are not certain, however, why this accessory began to be associated with witches.

In literature, the witch's frequent companion is the black cat. Black cats and other animals were long thought to perform witches' tasks. These animals, called familiars, were said to be low-ranking demons that assumed any animal shape, such as a toad, dog, insect, or black cat. People began to consider witches' familiars evil around the Middle Ages.

CHAPTER TWO

WITCHY HISTORY

Much witchcraft lore can be traced back to actual historical events. In fact, records of belief in witchcraft date back to prehistoric times. There is no single description that applies to witches in all societies that have believed in them. In the West, they are most often thought of as crones or hags—ugly old women. However, references to beautiful young female witches and to male witches exist, too.

WITCHCRAFT THROUGHOUT HISTORY

The earliest accounts of witchcraft are rooted in religion and mythology. There are several references to sorcerers

n the background of this painting, King Saul commits suicide after hearing the misfortune hat awaited him in his future from the Witch of Endor. Witches gather in the foreground.

in the Hebrew Bible, where they are condemned and their offenses are punishable by death. However, in the First Book of Samuel, King Saul asks the Witch of Endor for help. She summons spirits and foretells his death.

Witchcraft is mentioned in the writings of the ancient Greek poet Homer. In the *Odyssey*, the hero Odysseus encounters the lovely witch Circe. She uses spells and potions to change humans into wolves, lions, and swine. Though the *Odyssey* is fiction, belief in sorcery and witchcraft was widespread in the ancient world.

In both ancient Greece and Rome, harmful magical practices were punished, which meant that "good" witchcraft was tolerated, if not permitted. This was a good thing for healers. Healers and witches have been intertwined throughout history. As long as the healers of ancient Greece and Rome did no harm, they were not prosecuted.

After the arrival of Christianity, attitudes toward witchcraft varied for several centuries. Many regarded it as superstition, but some church leaders labeled it as evil. In the 11th century, however, positions toward witchcraft began to change. The Western perception of witchcraft transformed, associating it with heresy and the devil.

EUROPEAN WITCH HUNTS

Over the course of a few hundred years, many thousands of people in Europe were tried and convicted of being witches, and tens of thousands were executed. Even though many clergy and judges in the Middle Ages were skeptical of accusations of witchcraft, the period 1300–1330 can be seen as the beginning of European witch trials. Witches were believed to reject Christianity, to worship and make pacts with the devil, and to employ demons to accomplish magical deeds. In 1374, Pope Gregory XI declared that all magic was done

The devil (left) and the people who follow him show their hatred of Christianity by stepping on the cross in this engraving from 1626.

with the aid of demons and was open to prosecution for heresy. By 1435–1450, the number of prosecutions had begun to rise sharply. Toward the end of the 15th century, two events stimulated the hunt for witches: Pope Innocent VIII's publication in 1484 of a decree condemning witchcraft and *Malleus maleficarum* ("The Hammer of Witches"), a 1486 handbook written by Heinrich Krämer and Jacob Sprenger that blamed witchcraft chiefly on women. Both Protestants and Roman Catholics participated in the witch hunts. The hunts were most severe from 1580 to 1630.

This engraving depicts actual "witch hunter" Matthew Hopkins. He may have been responsible for the killing of around 300 women between the years 1644 and 1646. Some were only thought guilty for owning a pet.

The witch hunts varied enormously in place and in time, but they were united by a common religious and legal worldview. The hunts were not pursuits of individuals already identified as witches but efforts to identify witches. The process began with suspicions and, occasionally, continued through rumors and accusations until a conviction was reached. In some places torture was used to get the accused to confess or to name accomplices. Alleged victims usually made the accusations. Successful prosecution of one witch sometimes led to a local hunt for others.

THE TRIALS

Because accusations and trials of witches took place in both church and regular courts, the law played at least as important a role as religion in the witch hunts. Local courts were more likely to be violent in their treatment of supposed witches. Local practices included pricking witches to see whether the devil had protected them from pain; searching for the "devil's mark," an oddly shaped mole or wart; and throwing the accused into a pond—if the person sank, he or she was innocent. However, where central authority was strong, convictions were fewer and sentences milder.

Three-fourths of European witch hunts occurred in western Germany, the Low Countries (Belgium, the Netherlands, and Luxembourg), France, northern Italy, and Switzerland. There were additional hunts in Spanish America, where the European pattern of accusations continued. In Mexico, the Franciscan friars linked indigenous religion and magic with the devil. Prosecutions for witchcraft in Mexico began in the 1530s, and by the 1600s, indigenous peasants were reporting pacts with the devil. Like the Spanish colonies, the English colonies repeated the European model of witch hunts with a few minor differences. The first hanging for witchcraft in New England

One of the Salem witch trials is shown here in a painting from the mid-1700s. Notice the accusing, pointing fingers wielded by some of the onlookers.

was in 1647. The most famous executions occurred a few decades later in the town of Salem (now in Massachusetts).

The decline of witch hunts, like their origins, was gradual. By the late 16th century, many prosperous and professional people in Western Europe were being accused, so leaders began to have a personal interest in slowing the hunts. The legal use of torture declined in the 17th and 18th centuries, and there was a general lessening of religious intensity. Prosecutions of witches in Austria, Poland, and Hungary took place as late as the 18th century. The last known execution for witchcraft was in Switzerland in 1782.

THE SALEM WITCH TRIALS

The Salem witch trials were proceedings held in 1692 in Salem, Massachusetts Bay Colony, that led to the hanging of nineteen suspected witches and the imprisonment of many others. It started in May in Salem Village (now Danvers, Massachusetts) with accusations by young girls against women in the community. A special court was convened, and the trials quickly created uncontrollable panic and widespread charges of witchcraft. Even the governor's wife was accused. However, community leaders began to cast doubt on the use of certain types of evidence. In October, the special court was dissolved, and the imprisoned were freed.

Though the number is often quoted as being higher, no more than about 110,000 persons were tried for witchcraft, and no more than 40,000 to 60,000 people were executed. On the whole, about three-fourths of convicted witches were female. Why so many? There are many theories, including those that point to the frequency of females as healers and the fact that the accused women were often in powerless positions, particularly women without men in the household. However, both men and women, young and old, were named "witches" throughout history.

CHAPTER THREE

WITCHCRAFT TODAY

Belief in traditional witchcraft persists in some parts of the world. Witchcraft is used to try to control events that are often not in human control as well as to make sense of these events. Witchcraft explains the problem posed when one seeks to

This modern image of a witch shows her screaming as she casts a spell.

25

understand why misfortune strikes oneself rather than someone else. It can be used to explain the inequalities of life. Several Asian and African societies today continue to harbor a belief in witchcraft.

MODERN BELIEFS

Modern beliefs in witchcraft vary greatly. In some cultures, witchcraft is thought to include both good, or protective, magic and bad, or destructive, magic. Medicine people or shamans—sometimes called "witch doctors"—are healers who may practice protective magic. Traditional and modern African leaders sometimes surround themselves with witch doctors, for example, and are themselves thought to possess supernatural power. Much evil is blamed on witchcraft. In many parts of Africa and Asia, witches are said to cause sickness, death, and natural disasters, as well as misfortunes such as job loss.

In some African cultures, witches are thought to assemble in covens, at graveyards or around a fire to feast on their victims' blood. However, other African peoples believe that witches act unconsciously. Unaware of the ill they cause, the witches are thought to be driven by powerful urges to act evilly. It is easy, therefore, for those accused of witchcraft to assume that they unknowingly did what is attributed to them. This—along with suggestion and torture—helps explain the widely reported confessions of guilt in Africa.

Among the Zande of the Congo and some other central African peoples, the source of the evil-working capacity is believed to be located in the witch's stomach. It can be activated merely by wishing someone ill and is thus a kind of unspoken curse. Zande also believe that spells and potions can produce evil deeds even more effectively.

Accused witches are still tortured and even murdered in some societies. Some Indian villages have a practice of making women accused of witchcraft pick up a silver coin with her hands from a tank filled with boiling oil. If her hands are burned, she is confirmed to be a witch. She is then forced to free victims from her curse and made to leave the village.

A shaman in the Gabonese Republic of Central Africa creates a potion, which he believes will have healing powers.

MAGIC AND REASON

Like ancient and early modern Europeans, modern Africans and Asians who believe in the reality of witchcraft do not lack the power of rational reasoning. For example, if one's home collapses because it was poorly constructed, no witch is needed to explain this. If a boat sinks because it has a hole, witchcraft is not responsible. Witchcraft enters the picture when rational knowledge fails. It is used to explain the diseases whose causes are unknown, the mystery of death, and strange misfortunes.

Some misfortunes, like shipwrecks, have obvious causes, while others remain a mystery. Witchcraft seems to hold answers to mysteries for some people.

A sick African may consult both a medical doctor and a witch doctor. The first treats the external symptoms, while the second is thought to uncover the hidden causes. Just as the sick person takes preventive measures prescribed by the medical doctor, he or she might also take steps against the supernatural. The person may, for example, wear amulets to guard against witchcraft.

WICCA AND NEO-PAGANISM

Some people in the Western world also practice witchcraft today. In the early 21st century, perhaps a few hundred thousand people located mostly in North America and Great Britain embraced the spiritual movements Wicca and Neo-Paganism. Wiccans practice nature worship and witchcraft but see it as a religion based on pre-Christian traditions of Northern and Western Europe. Wiccans call themselves "witches." However, their ethical code directs them to do no harm to others. Wiccans do not worship the devil or evil spirits.

Neo-Paganism includes several movements that attempt to revive pre-Christian religions of Europe and the Middle East. These movements draw upon ancient polytheistic religions, or religions based on the worship of many gods. Neo-Paganism incorporates ritual practices into its tradition, but many Neo-Pagans prefer to think of themselves as practicing magic rather than religion. Although their emphasis is on opening themselves to hidden powers through rituals, chants, or charms, most Neo-Pagans do not call themselves "witches." Both Wiccans and Neo-Pagans tend to have strong ecological and environmental concerns, and they celebrate the change of seasons.

It is important to note that Wiccans and Neo-Pagans would likely have been condemned in the heyday of the witch hunts. Though they do not encourage violence or evil magic, their countercultural beliefs would have made them outcasts in their communities—and perhaps marked for execution for heresy and witchcraft.

This photograph shows one participant in a coven of Wiccans gathered in New York to perform ceremonies and rituals.

SCRUTINIZING SALEM

Modern historians and other scholars continue to study the witch hunts of the 14th to 18th centuries to try to figure out what happened and why. In the case of the Salem witch trials, records indicate that the accusations were initiated after two girls began behaving strangely. The pair had convulsions and claimed they were being pinched or bitten by unseen forces. The condition of the two girls seemed to spread, as several teenage girls in the community began having convulsive fits. The local doctor, rather than finding a medical reason, declared

The Witch House is the only building still standing from the witch trial period in Salem, Massachusetts. Judge Jonathan Corwin, who helped convict many villagers of witchcraft, lived here.

31

that the girls were under a spell. The two girls accused three women of practicing witchcraft against them. One of the women, a slave named Tituba, was beaten to force her to confess. When she admitted to communicating with the devil, panic erupted.

TROUBLE AT A HIGH SCHOOL

Some people believe that the girls in the Salem witch cases who claimed to be bewitched actually suffered from conversion disorder, a condition in which stress causes physical symptoms such as twitching. In rare cases, the symptoms can spread, in what is sometimes called mass psychogenic illness. In this illness, symptoms generally spread among a close-knit group of people, such as a circle of friends or group of factory workers, who believe they could fall similarly ill. The condition continues to afflict people.

Conversion disorder may explain the bizarre situation that occurred in the small town of Le Roy, New York, in 2011. More than a dozen high school girls began experiencing tics, twitches, and spasms. Later, a young man and an older woman were affected by similar symptoms. Doctors examined them all, but the results were inconclusive. Many said the physical symptoms were a result of conversion disorder.

Theories vary today about what was really wrong with the girls. Some people say they were simply seeking attention. Others believe they had a condition called conversion disorder (formerly called hysteria), in which anxiety is "converted" into physical symptoms, such as convulsions. Conversion disorder and epilepsy were two illnesses frequently **confused with witchcraft back then. Some people think the "bewitched" girls of Salem were poisoned by bad grain. A fungus called ergot can grow on grains and, when consume**d, can cause hallucinations, convulsions, and other effects.

rgot fungus, the black formations on this rye plant, can cause physical and mental problems hen consumed.

After the panic broke out, other people in the Salem community began accusing their neighbors of witchcraft. Many people think that the accusers were fueled by jealousy, anger, and fear. Accusations of witchcraft over the years have been used to strip people of power and possessions, to take revenge for past wrongs, to avoid being accused oneself, and to punish people for being different. More than likely, the events of Salem in the 1690s were brought about by a number of factors, a combination of church politics, feuds, and whatever condition affected the two girls.

CHAPTER FOUR

WITCHES IN POP CULTURE

Witchcraft continues to exercise a powerful hold on many people's imaginations. People remain fascinated by the possibility that someone may be able to possess supernatural powers, perhaps because they often feel powerless to influence events in their own lives. Equally as intriguing, however, is the idea that people would believe they are being manipulated by magic and accuse others of wielding witchcraft at them. Both these facets of witchcraft have been explored in many ways in Western popular culture. Witches remain a frequent focus of literature, television shows, and films.

WITCHES IN THE PAGES

Witches and witchcraft have appeared in numerous cultures' folklore, such as that collected and published by the Brothers Grimm. The witches who threatened Hansel and Gretel, Rapunzel, and other innocent characters are featured in some of the first thrilling bedtime stories that Western children hear.

The witches of the movie *The Wizard of Oz* (1939) were based on *The Wonderful Wizard of Oz*, a book by L. Frank Baum, published in 1900. Many sequels followed. Gregory Maguire's *Wicked: The Life and Times of the Wicked Witch of the West*, published in 1995, is a sympathetic look at the Wicked Witch of the West from the Oz tales. The story became a Broadway musical.

In British literature, the White Witch is a fearful character in C.S. Lewis's *The Chronicles of Narnia* book series of the 1950s. In Roald Dahl's *The Witches*, published in 1983, a young boy takes on the horrible witches

Harry Potter (right) and his friends were selected to attend Hogwarts, a special school to learn how to wield their magical powers—and battle the forces of evil in the world.

of England. In the *Harry Potter* series of books, published in 1997–2007, Potter and his friends attend the Hogwarts School of Witchcraft and Wizardry, encountering both benevolent and malevolent witches in their adventures.

WITCHES AND HALLOWEEN

Witches are a favorite Halloween costume. This may be because of Halloween's roots. The Celts of ancient Britain and Ireland had a three-day celebration at the beginning of November. They believed that spirits of the dead roamed

Witches continue to fascinate people of all ages. They inspire imaginations, especially around Halloween.

on the last night of October. In ancient Rome, the festival of Pomona, goddess of fruits and gardens, occurred around this time of year. It was an occasion of rejoicing associated with the harvest, but ghosts and witches were thought to be on the prowl. Even after November 1 became a Christian day for honoring saints, many people clung to the old beliefs and customs that had grown up about Halloween. Halloween is a great feast for Wiccans today.

MOVIE AND TV MAGIC

Many books involving witchcraft became successful movies. The *Harry Potter* films (2001–2011) are the highest-earning movie series to date. Other movies of note include *Oz the Great and Powerful* (2013), which tells the story of events before *The Wizard of Oz* (1939). *Snow White and the Huntsman* (2012) is a retelling of Snow White's conflict with her wicked stepmother, a powerful sorceress. Similarly, *Maleficent* (2014) relates the story of the queen who enchanted Sleeping Beauty.

On television, *Bewitched*, from the 1960s and early '70s, and *Charmed*, *Sabrina the Teenage Witch*, and *Buffy the Vampire Slayer*, all from the late 1990s and early 2000s, were long-running television shows with

Actress Angelina Jolie portrays Maleficent, an evil witch who is more than she seems, in the 2014 movie of the same name.

characters who were witches. *Witches of East End*, a TV series that began in 2013, focuses on a family of witches in a fictional seaside town. *Once Upon a Time*, which began airing in 2011, revisits some famous fairy tale characters, including the Wicked Witch of the West, with a new spin on the old stories.

THE CRUCIBLE

The famous play and later movie *The Crucible* is a partly fictional examination of the events of the Salem witch trials. This four-act play by Arthur Miller was first performed and published in 1953. Though set in 1692, *The Crucible* is actually a commentary on events in American politics during the 1950s. During this period, U.S. Senator Joseph McCarthy accused many Americans of being communist spies, destroying reputations and spreading fear. It was a modern witch hunt. The word "witch hunt" today can mean the act of unfairly looking for and harassing people who are accused of having unpopular opinions.

MYSTERY AND MAGIC CONTINUE

Helen Duncan became infamous as "Scotland's last witch" when she was charged in 1944 under the Witchcraft Act of 1735 for claiming to have the powers of a witch. Duncan said she could talk to the dead—and many believed her. In 1941, she maintained that she spoke to a missing sailor, informing the man's family that his ship had been sunk. Several months later, the British military revealed that the

Witches remain favorite characters in the popular imagination. In a typical pop culture image, a cackling green-skinned witch flies on a broomstick at night.

ship had indeed sank. In 1944, Duncan was convicted and went to jail for a short time. It is sometimes claimed that she was imprisoned because authorities feared she was about to disclose information about the upcoming D-Day landing of June 1944, another event the British wanted to keep secret. But how would Duncan know about this or the sailor's death?

People may never tire of speculating about witches and witchcraft, just as they never tire of donning witch and wizard costumes on Halloween. Similar to how many people wonder if aliens are out there in the universe, there will be those who wonder if some people here on Earth possess supernatural powers that they use for good or evil.

GLOSSARY

ARCHAIC Old and no longer in everyday use.

BEWITCH To use magic to make someone do, think, or say something.

COMMUNIST A person who believes in communism or is a member of a political party that supports communism, a political theory in which property and wealth is shared by a society.

CONVULSION A sudden violent shaking of the muscles in one's body that one is unable to control.

COVEN A group of witches.

DIVINATION The practice that seeks to foresee future events or discover hidden knowledge usually by the interpretation of omens or by the aid of supernatural powers.

EPILEPSY A disorder of the nervous system that can cause people to suddenly become unconscious and to have violent, uncontrolled movements of the body.

ETHICAL Relating to or involving questions of right and wrong.

HALLUCINATION The perception of something (such as an image, a sound, or a smell) that seems real but does not really exist and that is usually caused by mental illness or the effect of a drug.

HERESY A belief or opinion that does not agree with the official belief or opinion of a particular religion.

INDIGENOUS Produced, living, or existing naturally in a particular region or environment.

LORE Knowledge or belief about a subject that has been handed down by word of mouth or in the form of stories.

MAORI A member of the original people of New Zealand.

POPULAR CULTURE Cultural activities or products such as movies, books, or music reflecting or aimed at the tastes of the masses of ordinary people in society, especially young people.

RECITATION The act of saying or repeating something out loud, especially for an audience.

SPECULATE To form ideas or theories about something, usually when there are many things not known about it.

SUPERNATURAL Unable to be explained by science or the laws of nature.

SYNONYMOUS Having the same meaning.

TIC A regularly repeated twitching movement of a muscle that cannot be controlled.

FOR FURTHER READING

Dowswell, Paul, and Susan Greenwood. *Witches & Wizards*. Wigston, England: Anness Publishing, 2011.

Ganeri, Anita, and David West. *Witches and Warlocks*. New York, NY: PowerKids Press, 2011.

Jeffrey, Gary. *Witches and Sorcerers: Tales of Magic*. New York, NY: Rosen Central, 2011.

Malam, John. *Witches*. Irvine, CA: QEB Publishing, 2010.

Marciniak, Kristin. *The Salem Witch Trials*. Ann Arbor, MI: Cherry Lake Publishing, 2013.

Mills, J. Elizabeth. *Witches in America*. New York, NY: Rosen Publishing, 2012.

Speare, Elizabeth George. *The Witch of Blackbird Pond*. New York, NY: Houghton Mifflin Harcourt, 2011.

Von Zumbusch, Amelie. *The True Story of the Salem Witch Hunts*. New York, NY: PowerKids Press, 2009.

WEBSITES

Because of the changing nature of Internet links, Rosen Publishing has developed an online list of websites related to the subject of this book. This site is updated regularly. Please use this link to access the list:

http://www.rosenlinks.com/UTP/Witch

INDEX